EASTWOODLIBRARY
TOWN CENTRE CAMPUS
EASTWOOD LANE
ROTHERHAM
S65 1E

10·99

**Anthony Burgess**

before the date below.

A Clockwork

D1421057

Bloomsbury Methuen Drama
An imprint of Bloomsbury Publishing Plc

B L O O M S B U R Y

LON          Rotherham College of Arts and Technology          DNEY

R88014

**Bloomsbury Methuen Drama**
An imprint of Bloomsbury Publishing Plc

| | |
|---|---|
| 50 Bedford Square | 1385 Broadway |
| London | New York |
| WC1B 3DP | NY 10018 |
| UK | USA |

**www.bloomsbury.com**

**Bloomsbury is a registered trade mark of Bloomsbury Publishing Plc**

First published in the United Kingdom by Hutchinson Ltd 1987
This edition published in the United Kingdom in 1998 by
Methuen Publishing Limited
Re-issued with a new cover 2012
Reprinted by Bloomsbury Methuen Drama 2013 (twice)

© The Estate of Anthony Burgess 2012

Anthony Burgess has asserted his right under the Copyright, Designs and
Patents Act, 1988, to be identified as author of this work.

All rights reserved. No part of this publication may be reproduced or
transmitted in any form or by any means, electronic or mechanical,
including photocopying, recording, or any information storage or retrieval
system, without prior permission in writing from the publishers.

No responsibility for loss caused to any individual or
organization acting on or refraining from action as a result of the
material in this publication can be accepted by Bloomsbury or the author.

All rights whatsoever in this play are strictly reserved and application
for performance etc. should be made before rehearsals by professionals
and by amateurs to David Higham Associates, 7th Floor, Waverley
House, 7-12 Noel Street, London, W1F 8GQ. No performance
may be given unless a licence has been obtained.

No rights in incidental music or songs contained in the work are hereby
granted and performance rights for any performance/presentation
whatsoever must be obtained from the respective copyright owners.

**British Library Cataloguing-in-Publication Data**
A catalogue record for this book is available from the British Library.

ISBN: PB: 978-0-4137-3590-4
ePUB: 978-1-4081-4098-7

**Library of Congress Cataloging-in-Publication Data**
A catalog record for this book is available from the Library of Congress.

Typeset by Country Setting, Kingsdown, Kent
Printed and bound by CPI Group (UK) Ltd, Croydon, CR0 4YY

# *A prefatory word*

The novel, properly novella, entitled *A Clockwork Orange* first appeared in the spring of 1962. I had written its first version in late 1960, when I was coming to the end of what the neurological specialists had assured my late wife would be my terminal year. My late wife broke the secret in time for me to work hard at providing some posthumous royalties for her. In the period in which I was supposed to be dying from an inoperable cerebral tumour, I produced the novels entitled *The Doctor is Sick, Inside Mr Enderby, The Worm and the Ring* (a reworking of an earlier draft), *One Hand Clapping, The Eve of Saint Venus* (an expansion in novella form of a discarded opera libretto) and *A Clockwork Orange* in a much less fantastic version than the one that was eventually published. This first version presented the world of adolescent violence and governmental retribution in the slang that was current at the time among the hooligan groups known as the Teddy boys and the Mods and Rockers. I had the sense to realise that, by the time the book came out, the slang would already be outdated, but I did not see clearly how to solve the problem of an appropriate idiolect for the narration. When, in early 1961, it seemed to me likely that I was not going to die just yet, I thought hard about the book and decided that its story properly belonged to the future, in which it was conceivable that even the easy-going British state might employ aversion therapy to cure the growing disease of youthful aggression. My late wife and I spent part of the summer of 1961 in Soviet Russia, where it was evident that the authorities had problems with turbulent youth not much different from our own. The *stilyagi*, or style-boys, were smashing faces and windows, and the police, apparently obsessed with ideological and fiscal crimes, seemed powerless to keep them under. It struck me that it might be a good idea to create a kind of young hooligan who bestrode the iron curtain and spoke an argot compounded of the two most powerful political languages in the world – Anglo-American and Russian. The irony of the style would lie in the hero-narrator's being totally unpolitical.

There was what must seem, to us who are living in a more permissive age, an unaccountable delay in getting the work accepted for publication. My literary agent was even dubious about submitting it to a publisher, alleging that its pornography of violence would be certain to make it unacceptable. I, or rather my late wife, whose Welsh blood forced her into postures of aggression on her husband's behalf, reminded the agent that it was his primary job not to make social or literary judgements on the work he handled but to sell it. So the novella was sold to William Heinemann Ltd in London. In New York it was sold to W. W. Norton Inc, though with the last chapter missing. To lop the final section of the story, in which the protagonist gives up his youthful violence in order to become a man with a man's responsibilities, seemed to me to be very harmful: it reduced the work from a genuine novel (whose main characteristic must always be a demonstration of the capacity of human nature to change) to a mere fable. Moreover, though this was perhaps a minor point, it ruined the arithmology of the book. The book was written in twenty-one chapters (21 being the symbol of human maturity) divided into three sections of exactly equal size. The American reduction looks lopsided. But the American publisher's argument for truncation was based on a conviction that the original version, showing as it does a capacity for regeneration in even the most depraved soul, was a kind of capitulation to the British Pelagian spirit, whereas the Augustinian Americans were tough enough to accept an image of unregenerable man. I was in no position to protest, except feebly and in the expectation of being overborne: I needed the couple of hundred dollars that comprised the advance on the work.

I was, in fact, very poor at the time, and my heart leapt with the expectation of becoming less poor when BBC television decided to devote part of their regular programme *Tonight* to a consideration of the book. There were only two television channels in those days, and the commercial one was more popular than the BBC, but *Tonight* was said to have at least nine million viewers, and I went to Lime Grove from my East Sussex village with visions of all the good the publicity would do. The first chapter of the book was very adequately dramatised, and then there was a long discussion on its language, theme and even theology. I travelled back from Charing Cross to Etchingham with my spirits higher than, in this damnable writing game, they had ever been before or have ever been since. Surely, I thought, at least one per cent of the nine million viewers would buy the book. But, no. It sold much worse than my very first novel. It had cleared three thousand copies by the next accounting day. It was, like much of my work, a financial failure. I learned a very profound lesson from that experience: never permit overexposure. The *Tonight* programme had told the viewers too much about the book: if they wanted to discuss it they knew enough without having to buy it. The reviews it received not only failed to whet an appetite among prospective book-buyers: they were for the most part facetious and uncomprehending. What I had tried to write was, as well as a novella, a sort of allegory of Christian free will. Man is defined by his capacity to choose courses of moral action. If he chooses good, he must have the possibility of choosing evil instead: evil is a theological necessity. I was also saying that it is more acceptable for us to perform evil acts than to be conditioned artificially into an ability and only to perform what is socially acceptable. The *Times Literary Supplement* reviewer (anonymous in those days) saw the book only as a 'nasty little shocker', which was rather unfair, while the down-market newspapers thought the Anglo-Russian slang was a silly little joke that didn't come off. I did not repine. I was learning to accept the indignities of the writer's life. I put *A Clockwork Orange* behind me and pushed on with other novels, as I still do.

But the nasty little shocker was gaining an audience, especially among the American young. Rock groups called

'Clockwork Orange' began to spring up in New York and Los Angeles. These juveniles were primarily intrigued by the language of the book, which became a genuine teenage argot, and they liked the title. They did not realise that it was an old Cockney expression used to describe anything queer, not necessarily sexually so, and they hit on the secondary meaning of an organic entity, full of juice and sweetness and agreeable odour, being turned into an automaton. The youth of Malaysia, where I had lived for nearly six years, saw that *orange* contained *orang*, meaning in Malay, a human being. In Italy, where the book became *Arancia all'Orologeria*, it was assumed that the title referred to a grenade, an alternative to the ticking pineapple. The small frame of the novella did not noticeably enrich me, but it led to a proposal that it be filmed. It was in, I think, 1965, that the rock group known as the Rolling Stones expressed an interest in the buying of the property and an acting participation in a film version which I myself should write. There was not much money in the project, because the permissive age in which crude sex and cruder violence could be frankly presented had not yet begun. If the film was to be made at all, it would have to be in a cheap underground version leased out to clubs. But it was not made. Not yet.

It was the dawn of the age of candid pornography that enabled Stanley Kubrick to exploit, to a serious artistic end, those elements in the story which were meant to shock morally rather than merely titillate. These elements are, to some extent, hidden from the reader by the language used: to *tolchock* a *chelloveck* in the *kishkas* does not sound so bad as booting a man in the guts, and the *old in-out in-out*, even if it reduces the sexual act to a mechanical action, does not sicken quite so much as a Harold Robbins description of cold rape. But in a film little can be implied; everything has to be shown. Language ceases to be an opaque protection against being appalled and takes a very secondary place. I was bound to have misgivings about the film, and one of the banes of my later life has been the public assumption that I had something to do with it. I did not. I wrote a script, like nearly everybody else in the script-writing world, but nobody's script was used. The book itself, as in a literary seminar, was taken on to the film set, discussed, sectionally dramatised with much free improvisation, and then, as film, stowed in the can. All that I provided was a book, but I had provided it ten years previously. The British state had ignored it, but it was not so ready to ignore the film. It was considered to be an open invitation to the violent young, and inevitably I was regarded as an antisocial writer. The imputation that I had something to do with the punk cult, whose stepfather I was deemed to be by *Time* magazine, has more to do with the gorgeous technicolor of Kubrick's film than with my own subfusc literary experiment.

I am disclosing a certain gloom about visual adaptation of my little book, and the reader has now the right to ask why I have contrived a stage version of it. The answer is very simple: it is to stem the flow of amateur adaptations that I have heard about though never seen. It is to provide a definitive actable version which has auctorial authority. And, moreover, it is a version which, unlike Kubrick's cinema adaptation, draws on the entirety of the book, presenting at the end a hooligan hero who is now growing up, falling in love, proposing a decent bourgeois life with a wife and family, and consoling us with the doctrine that aggression is an aspect of adolescence which maturity rejects. This is not, of course, altogether true: our football assassins are presumably grown men, but there is something about football which restores the mindlessness of adolescence: grown men should have something better to do than watch a ball being kicked around. This view will make me unpopular with intellectual fans like Sir Freddie Ayer, but I sincerely hold it. Alex the hero speaks for me when he says in effect that destruction is a substitute for creation, and that the energy of youth has to be expressed through aggression because it has not yet been able to subdue itself through creation. Alex's aggressive instincts have been stimulated by classical music, but the music has been forewarning him of what he must some day become: a man who recognises the Dionysiac in, say, Beethoven but appreciates the Apollonian as well.

It is appropriate that the music chosen for the setting of my harmless little lyrics should be derived from Beethoven. There are three numbers which call for music of my own, or somebody else's, but the Beethoven spirit must be here – the spirit of the mature creative mind which can reconcile the creative and the destructive. Beethoven is long out of copyright and may be freely banged around on a piano with whatever percussion suggests itself. This is not grand opera. It is a little play which any group may perform, and it is my farewell to a preoccupation which has continued too long. I mean an enforced concern with a book which belongs very much to my past – after all, it is all of a quarter of a century old – and which I would prefer to forget. I have written other books and, I think, better ones.

One final point. I toyed, when first publishing the book, with the notion of affixing an epigraph from Shakespeare. This was considered to be a dangerously literary proposal: the book had to stand naked with no chaperonage from the Bard. But perhaps I may now conclude with it. In Act III Scene 3 of *The Winter's Tale*, the shepherd who finds the child Perdita says: 'I would there were no age between ten and three-and-twenty, or that youth would sleep out the rest; for there is nothing in the between but getting wenches with child, wronging the ancientry, stealing, fighting –.' It sounds like an exceptionally long adolescence, but perhaps Shakespeare was thinking of his own. It is the adolescence, somewhat briefer, that I present in *A Clockwork Orange*.

Anthony Burgess
Lugano, July 1986

EASTWOOD LIBRARY
ACC NO R88014
DATE 21.09.17
CLASS 822.914
BUR

# A Clockwork Orange

LANCHESTER LIBRARY
ACC No.
DATE
CLASS

This dramatised version of *A Clockwork Orange* was first presented by Northern Stage at the Newcastle Playhouse, Newcastle-upon-Tyne, in September 1998 with the following cast:

Francisco Alfonsin          Jan Birkett
Mark Calvert                Maggie Carr
Craig Conway                Alex Elliot
Joanna Holden               Rebecca Hollingsworth
Stephen Lamb                Mark Lloyd
Tony Neilson                Darren Palmer
Peter Peverley

*Directed by* Alan Lyddiard and Mark Murphy
*Designed by* Neil Murray
*Lighting by* Jon Linstrum
*Music arranged and composed by* John Alder
*Film by* Mark Murphy

# Act One

*It is a winter night sometime in the unforeseeable future. It is not clear where we are, but it is obviously a capital city. The winking electric sign of the Korova Milk Bar, with the word MOLOKO, shows that this could be beyond the iron curtain, since the letters are Cyrillic. This, on the other hand, may be signmaker's whimsy. From this milk bar come four boys, dressed fantastically in a style of extreme machismo. They are* **Alex**, **Georgie**, **Pete** *and* **Dim**. *These names could conceivably be Russian, with* **Dim** *an abbreviation for* **Dimitri**. *Their true nation is that of the teenager, whom, using Russian, they would call the Nadsat. Their slang too is to be termed Nadsat. As they are friends we will designate them with the Russian word drug, which, wrongly, they pronounce droog. It means friend. They sing, freely adapting the Scherzo of Beethoven's Ninth Symphony.*

**Droogs**
What's it going to be then, eh?
What's it going to be then, eh?
Tolchocking, dratsing and kicks in the yarblockos,
Thumps on the gulliver, fists in the plott.
Gromky great shooms to the bratchified millicent,
Viddy the krovvy pour out of his rot.
Ptitsas and cheenas and starry babushkas
– A crack in the kishkas real horrorshow hot.
Give it them whether they want it or not.

*A* **Man**, *evidently high on drugs, totters out of the milk bar. He looks up at the moon and burbles.*

**Man**     Aristotle wishy washy works outing cyclamen get forficulate smartish. Shine shine O antepenultimate in gross bladderwrack follicles.

*The droogs laugh in derision.* **Dim** *prepares to crack him one but* **Alex** *the leader intervenes.*

**Alex**     In the land. In orbit. Stoned into a balloon. Alone with Bog and all his holy angels and saints. Very nice but

very like cowardly. You were not put on this earth just to get
into touch with Bog. That sort of thing can sap all the
strength and goodness out of a malchick.

**Man**    Fret not in unfrellicated arbuckles. Let grollibated
urchins frolic in left right front back ilfracombes. Work.
Garnish celibate. Off. Out. Waaaaah.

*He totters off. The droogs' song resumes.*

**Droogs**
    What's it going to be then, eh?
    Deng in our carmans so no need for crasting
    And making the gollybird cough up its guts.
    Tolchocks and twenty-to-one in an alleyway,
    Rookers for fisting and britvas for cuts.
    What's it going to be then, eh?
    As one door closes another one shuts.
    Govoreet horrorshow, but me no buts.

*The four march off whistling the trio from the scherzo of Beethoven's
Ninth as the lights of the milk bar wink out. They turn as noise
approaches.* **Billyboy** *and his gang appear, dragging a screaming*
**Girl**. **Alex** *is delighted.*

**Alex**    Well, if it isn't fat stinking billygoat Billyboy in
poison. How are thou, thou globby bottle of cheap grazzy
chip oil? Come and get one in the yarbles, if you have any
yarbles, you eunuch jelly, thou.

*The knives and bicycle chains come out. The* **Girl** *makes her getaway,
running off screaming. There is now a fight, very exactly choreographed
to music.* **Dim** *is the most vigorous but least stylish of the four droogs.
The gang of* **Billyboy** *limps off, slashed, bloody.* **Alex** *looks
critically at* **Dim**.

**Alex**    Viddy yourself, O Dim. Your platties a grahzny
mess and red red krovvy on your litso. That I like not.

**Dim**    What thou likest I care not, bratty. Profound shooms
of lip-music to thee and thine.

**Alex**    Govoreet not thuswise, O Dim, to him that is your rightful leader.

**Dim**    Yarbles. Bolshy great yarblockos.

**Alex** *prepares to move on to* **Dim** *with his threatening razor, but* **Georgie** *steps in.*

**Georgie**    What's this of a leader? You Alexander the bolshy then? We govoreeted not before of a leader. It was all for one before and all droogs together. Right? Rightiright?

**Pete**    Oh, very much rightiright.

**Alex**    Wrong, Pete. Wrong, Georgie. (*He sings.*)

There's got to be
Some one in charge.
Who do you see?
Him?
Dim the dim?
Or me –
Alex the large?

There's those that come
Ripe for the job
Some are like scum
You?
You won't do.
Pete's dumb.
Georgie's a slob.

Don't govoreet a slovo, you and you –
Not one shoom from your rot.
You pony that it's pravda, pravda, true –
Isn't it not?

There's some get born
Horned like a ram.
Who blows the horn?
Me.
Me, not he or thou or thee,

You little shorn
Lamb.
I am the bolshy big-big-balled I am.

*The others prepare to say something, but* **Alex**, *as leader, indicates that somebody has arrived. Two people, in fact –* **P. Alexander** *and his* **Wife**. *She is young, pretty; he is older, more scholarly. He carries a leather folder. They are hurrying somewhere. The droogs get in their way.*

**Alex**   A real dobby evening to thee and thine, O brother and sister. Ah, real horrorshow ochkies.

*He means* **Alexander**'s *glasses, which he pulls off and smashes on the ground.* **Alexander** *makes noises of protest, his* **Wife** *starts to hit out with her handbag. This amuses the four droogs.* **Alex** *grabs the leather case and takes out a mass of manuscript.*

**Alex**   Never fear. If fear thou hast in thy heart, O brother, pray banish it forthwith. What is this? (*Fiercely.*) *What is it?*

**Alexander**   A b – A b – A bbb –

**Alex**   A book. It's a book what you have written of. I have ever had the most bezoomny admiration for them as can write books, brother. And the name is Alexander, the same as mine. There's a cohen sidence. *A Clockwork Orange.* A fair gloopy title. Who ever heard of a clockwork orange? 'The attempt to impose upon man, a creature of growth and capable of sweetness, to ooze juicily at the last round the bearded lips of God, to attempt to impose, I say, laws and conditions appropriate only to a mechanical creation – against this I raise my sword-pen.'

*He sings this in the form of an operatic recitative. The man and woman are held by the other three while he does so. They struggle soundlessly, both having their mouths stuffed by the balled-up typescript,* **Alex** *singing only from the first page. And now the man is left for near-dead on the ground while his* **Wife** *is, God help her, prepared for –* The *droogs sing to the melody of the second movement of Beethoven's Sonata Pathétique:*

**Alex**

In and out –
We love the old in-out.

**Others** (*accompanying*)

In out in out in out in out . . .

**Alex**

We push, pull, leaving no trace,
Like rowers in a boat race.
(*The song accelerates.*)
In and out –
Until the final shout.

**Others** (*as before*)

In out in out in out in out . . .

**Alex**

You'll know soon what it's not for:
We're going to give you what for.

*The lights dim as they take the struggling girl off. Manic music. It dies down. The lights go up to show the Korova sign blinking backwards. We are inside the milk bar. The four droogs, tired, drink milk.*

**Alex**    Fagged and shagged and fashed and bashed.

*A song comes out of the loudspeaker. An emasculated voice, that of Johnny Zhivago, warbles:*

You blister my paint,
Make me feel faint.
It's slaughter.
You turn my knees to water.
Water you ain't.

When I shove my saint
Into your quaint
Cathedral,
I get all tetrahedral,
Got no restraint.

*It is* **Dim** *who has put this song on the invisible jukebox. He prances around, fingerclicking. But a different music is to be heard from a dark corner. It is a sweet girl's voice singing the theme from the fourth movement of Beethoven's Ninth. The lights go up to show her and a small group with vocal scores in their hands. They drink milk.*

## The Girl

> Joy thou glorious spark of heaven,
> Daughter of Elysium,
> Hearts on fire, aroused, enraptured,
> To thy sacred shrine we come.
> Custom's bond no more can sever
> Those by thy sure magic tied.
> All mankind are loving brothers
> Where thy sacred wings abide.

**Alex** *is enchanted. He cries out at* **Dim**.

**Alex**    Off with that cal. This is like real music.

**Dim** *makes contemptuous noises.* **Alex** *gets up and goes off. We hear the pop song stop and the sound of smashed glass.* **Dim** *fights the returning* **Alex**, *but the latter, all ears for the music, gives him one thump in the belly which makes him double up. The Beethoven ends,* **Alex** *claps. A man emerges from the music group. It is* **Mr Deltoid**. *He is young though ageing through the stress of his job, which is that of probation officer. He goes up to* **Alex**.

**Deltoid**    Little Alex, yes. Sick this morning so no school. Sick tomorrow morning too so the same, yes. But very fit and well in the night, yes?

**Alex**    Mr Deltoid, sir. I am surprised to see you in a mesto of this like depravity.

**Deltoid**    Depravity, eh? To me it looks very much like a harmless milk bar. But I hear that the white milk can be a harmless wrapper for certain drugs, such as drencrom, vellocet and the like, yes?

**Alex**    Terrible, sir. Drugs, sir, can sap all the strength and goodness out of a malchick. Them I touch not, oh no verily not.

**Deltoid**    No, yes. Have to keep up our strength and badness to indulge in crimes of the night, don't we? I and my friends create. We are here to quench our wholesome thirst after an evening's music. But you destroy, don't you? (*He bangs* **Alex** *at each key word.*) Destroy, yes? Break. Steal. Commit mayhem. Slash. Soon you will kill, yes?

**Alex***'s droogs clearly enjoy this, the leader being visibly rebuked.* **Dim** *lets out loud lip shooms.* **Alex** *is humiliated.*

**Alex**    Never, sir. Never not. Life is like sacred, Mr Deltoid, sir.

**Deltoid**    This I say to you, little Alex. The next time it will not be the Corrective School. Next time it will be the barry hole. All my work ruined. My prospects of promotion frustrated. Remember that, yes. And I will not speak up for you, oh no. I will say that you are villainy incarnate. I will say that you are Original Sin prowling the town. I will sing loud and clear.

*He sings now:*

    What gets into you all?
    Theological evil?
    The devil stalking the street?
    The weevil in the flour of life?
    I repeat:
    What gets into you all?

**Alex**    Nobody's got nothing on me, sir. I've been out of the rookers of the millicents for a long time now.

**Deltoid**    That's just what worries me. A bit too long of a time to be healthy. You're about due now by my reckoning. That's why I'm warning you, little Alex, to keep your handsome young proboscis out of the dirt, yes. Do I make myself clear?

**Alex**    As an unmuddied lake, sir. Clear as an azure sky of
deepest summer.

*The song is resumed, but it has become a duet.*

| **Alex** | **Deltoid** |
|---|---|
| What gets into us all? | What gets into you all? |
| Theological evil, prrrrrr. | Theological evil? |
| The devil stalking the street, prrr. | The devil stalking the street? |
| The weevil in the flour of life, prrr. | The weevil in the flour of life. |
| Don't repeat: | I repeat: |
| What gets into us all? | What gets into you all? |

**Alex**

Let me explain, to you, oh my brothers.
As for him and the others
It's no good saying a word to them – It's never occurred to
    them that
Energy's something built into a boy,
But neither the church nor the state
Has taught us how to create,
So we've got to use energy to destroy.
Destruction's our ode to joy.

**Deltoid**

What gets into you all?
Is it biological? Drivel!
It's unambivalent sin.
It's the devil grinning within.
God help us all.

**Deltoid**, *shaking his head, goes back to his companions, who leave
the milk bar singing Ode to Joy in unison.* **Alex**'s *droogs taunt him.*

**Pete**    No, Mr Deltoid, sir. Yes, Mr Deltoid, sir. Alex the
not so large.

**Dim**    You shouldn't have done what you done to me,
bratty. That tolchock in the kishkas. Not having that I'm
not.

*He draws his razor and advances on* **Alex**. **Alex** *draws his. The two warily stalk each other.* **Alex** *strikes* **Dim**'s *wrist.* **Dim** *drops his razor and howls, sucking blood.*

**Alex**   Anybody else interessovatted in a bit of fillying? Eh? Good. Dobby. Rightiright. We proceed, under the like leadership of your little droog Alex, to the next veshch of the nochy. Right, Dim? Right, Georgie? Rightiright, O Pete of my heart?

*His droogs reluctantly nod or say 'Right'. Singing the Ode to Joy,* **Alex** *leads them off. The light dims and comes up again. Music continues. The light comes up on an interior. The most notable content is a table with a bust of Beethoven on it. The doorbell is ringing. An* **Old Lady** *hobbles on and hobbles towards the ringing. It is* **Pete**'s *voice that we hear from outside. The* **Old Lady** *waves her stick at the voice.*

**Old Lady**   What is it? Who is it?

**Pete** (*off*)   An accident, madam. My friend has just been knocked down by a bus. Please let me in to telephone for an ambulance. Please. Please – he's like dying. (*We hear* **Dim**'s *simulated groan.*)

**Old Lady**   I know your tricks, boy. Smelly little bedbugs. Coming to make trouble for *real* people. Be off with you or I'll ring the police.

**Alex** *leaps in behind her as from a window.*

**Alex**   No phoning tonight, missis. I have taken the inestimable and detestable trouble of cutting the phone off – see, with my little britva.

*She has turned in fright, but she gamely raises her stick.*

**Old Lady**   Out of here. I've had too much of it. First one war and then another war with the bombs dropping. I won't have you as well. I'll die peaceful.

**Alex**   Die in your own good time, you grahzny starry forella. All I desire is like share and share alike like. Me and my droogs have a malenky dollop of nichevo. Jobless, ah yes. Not one lomtick of deng in our empty carmans. You and yours have built the grahzny world we like live in. So now you pay. Yes yes, pay. (*He sees the bust of Beethoven.*) Ah – Ludwig van that I love. Lovely lovely and all for me. With that I start.

*He makes for the bust. She raises her stick and cracks him feebly.* **Alex** *speaks with regret.*

**Alex**    Ah, not having that we're not, ah no.

*She continues to hit out at him. Incensed, he cracks her on the head with the bust of Beethoven. She makes desperate noises and goes down.* **Alex** *kicks at her but she does not move. Frightened, he makes for the door. He opens it and his three droogs move in.*

**Dim**    Not right what you did, little bratty. Just time, just time to make like our ittying off. The rozzes are on their way. Ah. Hear that lovely shoom?

*He means the hee-hawing of a police car. He raises his bicycle chain and whips* **Alex** *across the eyes.* **Alex** *moans, blinded. The droogs leave.* **Alex** *hears the Ode to Joy being sung as before, off, in the street.*

**Alex**    Mr Deltoid, sir. Help me. You're my friend, sir. Mr Deltoid.

*But the noise of the police car is loud. It stops. Three* **Policemen** *come in. One of them goes at once to the battered old lady on the floor. The others address* **Alex**.

**Policeman 1**    Well, if it isn't little Alex all to our own selves.

**Alex**    I did nothing. It was my treacherous droogs. They like framed me, brothers. Knocked out this old forella and then me. The pain in my glazzies is killing.

**Policeman 2**    A real pleasure this is. Not often we has the like privilege. (*He delivers a gentle thump.*)

**Alex**    I'm blind, Bog bust and bleed you, you grahzny bastards.

**Policeman 1**     Language, language (*He too thumps.*)

**Alex**     Bog murder you, you vonny stinking bratchnies. Where are the others? Where are my stinking traitorous droogs? It was all their idea, brothers. They like forced me to do it. I'm innocent, Bog butcher you.

**Policeman 3** *has been rendering artificial respiration to the* **Old Lady**. He gets up shaking his head.

**Policeman 3**     I think she's had it. Can't be sure, need the doctor. Phone from the car.

*He goes out, meeting* **Deltoid** *coming in.*

**Policeman 3**     Evening, Mr Deltoid. He must be a big disappointment to you.

**Deltoid**     Evening evening, yes. So it's happened, Alex boy, yes? Just as I thought it would. Dear dear, yes. So now he gets out of my soft probationary gloves into the calloused paws of the law. Yes. Well, this is the end of the line for me, yes. I suppose I'll have to be in court tomorrow.

**Alex**     It wasn't me, sir, brother. Speak up for me, sir, for I'm not so bad. I was led on by the treachery of the others, sir.

**Policeman 1**     Sings like a linnet. Sings the roof off lovely, he does that.

**Deltoid**     I'll speak. I'll be there tomorrow, yes, fear not.

**Policeman 2**     If you'd like to give him a bash in the chops, sir, don't mind us. We'll hold him down. He must be another great disappointment to you.

**Deltoid** *goes up to* **Alex** *and spits in his eye, spits full and lovely.* **Alex** *takes out his tashtook to wipe off the spit. While this is happening a* **Police Doctor**, *accompanied by* **Policeman 3** *comes in. He takes out his stethoscope and examines the* **Old Lady**.

**Alex**     Thank you, sir. Thank you very much, sir, that was real horrorshow. Did my hurt glazzies a lot of like good, sir, like the spit of the bearded veck that they hung on the cross on the halt and the lame. All right. Tonight you can have it all. A signed confession, right right right. I'm not going to crawl around no more, you merzky gets. You can have it all – dratsing and fillying and tolchocking and the old in-out, the lot.

**Policeman 3**    It looks like you can add a new one, right, doc?

*The* **Doctor** *nods gravely.* **Alex**, *who can see now, realizes what he has done.*

**Alex**    Snuffed it, has she? Well, well, real horrorshow.

**Policeman 3**    Horrorshow is right.

**Alex**    And me only just gone fourteen.

*The scene ends.*

*The lights come up on the* **Prison Chaplain**, *who stands, with a lectern, facing the audience, which we must imagine is a group of prisoners in the prison chapel. There is a hymn being sung and the* **Chaplain**, *and the* **Warders** *who stand behind him, shout threats and objurgations into the auditorium.*

*The Hymn*
> Weak tea are we, new-brewed,
> But stirring make all strong.
> We eat no angel's food,
> Our time of trial is long.
> But may we all begin
> To curse the strength of sin
> And all the devil's brood
> And let thy goodness in. Amen.

**Warders**    Stop talking there, bastards. I'm watching you, 920573. One on the turnip coming up for you, filth. Just you wait, 7749222.

**Chaplain**    Louder, damn you, sing up.

*He takes a swig of Scotch and a puff from a cigar before sailing into his sermon.*

**Chaplain**    What's it going to be then, eh? Is it going to be in and out and in and out of penal institutions, though more in than out for most of you, or are you going to attend to the divine word and realize the punishments that await the unrepentant sinner in the next world as well as in this? A lot of blasted idiots you are, selling your birthright for a saucer of cold porridge. The thrill of theft, of violence, the urge to live easy – is it worth it when we have proof, undeniable proof, incontrovertible evidence that hell exists? I know, I know, my friends, I have been informed in visions that there is a place, darker than any prison, hotter than any flame of human fire, where souls of unrepentant sinners like yourselves – and don't leer at me, damn you, don't laugh – like yourselves, I say, scream in endless and intolerable agony, their noses choked with the stink of filth, their mouths crammed with burning ordure, their skin rotting and peeling, a fireball spinning in their screaming guts. Yes yes, I know, *I know.* Remember. Now go. May the Holy Trinity keep you always and make you good, amen.

*He takes another draw and a swig while the* **Warders** *march off. The music of the voluntary is Bach's Choral Prelude* 'Wachet Auf'. **Alex** *now comes on, in prison dress. He is otherwise much what he was, though he has learned the art of hypocrisy. He carries a well-thumbed Bible.*

**Chaplain**    Thank you as always, little 6655321. The music you chose was, as always, admirable. Taste is a great thing. It leads one to the beautiful, and beauty, with truth and goodness, is one of the attributes of God.

**Alex**    Music is heaven, sir, I see that. Beyond this horrible world of evil. I do so want goodness too, and that's the truth.

**Chaplain**    The truth is in that holy book you handle, little 6655321. I am overjoyed that you read it. There is a text I would in particular ask you to ponder on.

*He grabs the Bible from* **Alex** *and looks carefully through it.*

**Chaplain**    I see you read the Old Testament more than the New. But it is in the New that the word of the Lord most scintillantly shines.

**Alex**    Too much govoreeting and preachifying, sir.

**Chaplain**    What's that, boy?

**Alex**    I love the preachifying, sir.

**Chaplain**    You have made notes here. What does this say? page 368 – 'Yahudies tolchocking each other real horrorshow and then wiping off the red red krovvy and spatting with their like handmaidens and peeting the old vino.' What is all this blasphemy about?

**Alex**    That was already in it when I got it, sir. Terrible. I wish I like understood it.

**Chaplain**    'I would like to be dressed in the heighth of like Roman fashion and tolchock the bearded nagoy veck all the way to his crucifixion.' Corruption, corruption. I must give you another copy. There are plenty around.

**Alex**    Sir, I've tried to be good, haven't I, sir? I've done my best, isn't that so? All of the two years I've been in, sir.

**Chaplain**    Go on as you are, little 6655321, and you will probably earn your remission.

**Alex**    But, sir, how about this new thing they're all talking about? How about this new like treatment that gets you out in no time at all and makes sure that you never get back in again?

**Chaplain**    Where did you hear this? Who's been telling you these things?

**Alex**    A bit of old newspaper gets blown in on the wind, or two warders talk as it might be. It's called the something or other whatsit, sir.

**Chaplain**    The Lodovico Technique. Yes. Of course, it's only in the experimental stage at the moment. It's very simple but very drastic.

**Alex**    But it's being used here, isn't it, sir? Those new like white buildings by the south wall. We've watched those being built, while we were doing our like exercise. Sir, that is.

**Chaplain**    It's not been used yet. Not in this prison, 6655321. Himself – the governor, that is – he has grave doubts about it. I must confess I share those doubts. The question is whether such a technique can make a man good. Goodness comes from within, 6655321. Goodness is something chosen. When a man cannot choose, he ceases to be a man.

*He would perhaps say more, but he is interrupted. A* **Warder** *marches on five prisoners –* **Zophar**, **The Doctor**, **Big Jew**, **Jojohn** *and* **Pedofil**. *They halt and face front. They carry brooms and order arms with them.*

**Warder**    Detail for chapel-cleaning all present and correct. *Sir!*

**Chaplain**    Very well. Think on these things, little 6655321.

*He goes out somewhat wearily, carrying his bottle of Scotch and the Bible. The* **Warder** *addresses the detail.*

**Warder**    Right, get down to it. (*To* **Pedofil**.) You, you're new here. I want to see work. This is only the chapel, but I want to see it clean as if it was the governor's toilet. Right?

**Pedofil**    Right, you say, but I want rights. Done more porridge than any of this lot and I know what's what. It's four to a cell, that's regulations, and there's six in this one. Have to sleep on the bleeding floor when that kid there has a bunk to his self. I demand my sodding rights.

**Warder**    Rights, is it? All the prisons is the same and it's you criminal bastards as is responsible.

**Pedofil**    Criminals. There's not one proper sodding criminal among the lot of them. That kid there, and he's a pox doctor and this one's on the con. I'm not having it. I demand my bleeding rights.

**Warder**    He wants his rights, lads. I'm just having a drag in that bog there. I think five minutes ought to do it.

*He goes out.* **Zophar** *nods and they all drop their brooms and start to knock about the newcomer. They also sing the following song:*

Discipline, discipline,
Let's have discipline,
Give him a haircut and shave.
Courtesy, deference –
That's with reference
To the foul way you behave.
The names you call us
Quite appal us –
We're going to knock you into shape.
You're going to suffer,
You duffed up duffer,
You jabbering gibbering ape.

Discipline, discipline,
Real live discipline,
Like what you get in a war.
When we've got through with you,
What can they do with you?
Use you for swabbing the floor.
You're going to college
To get some knowledge
Of how to behave and how.
So here comes discipline, discipline, discipline,
Here comes discipline now.

*But* **Pedofil** *is clearly not well. He cries 'Art! Art!' meaning 'Heart!' He receives a hard boot in the guts from* **Jojohn** *and goes down moaning on the floor.* **Alex** *has been comparatively unviolent.* **The Doctor** *gets down and listens for a heartbeat when the moaning* *ceases. He gets up shaking his head sadly. He looks sadly at* **Alex**. *So then do the others.*

**The Doctor**   You shouldn't have gone for him like that, my boy. It was most ill-advised. I could see from the colour of his lips that he had a heart condition.

**Alex**   Me? I hardly touched the bratchny. You weren't backward in putting it in, Doc. What you all viddying me like that for?

**Big Jew**   Alekth, you were too impetuouth. That latht kick wath a very very nathty one.

**Alex**   It was *his* tolchock – him there. You all viddied it.

**The Doctor**   Nobody will deny having a little kick at the man, to teach him a salutary lesson so to speak, but it's apparent that you, my dear boy, with the forcefulness and, and, shall I say, heedlessness of youth, dealt him the coo de grass. It's a great pity.

**Alex**'*s anger is considerable. He cries aloud.*

**Alex**   Traitors. Traitors and liars. Is the whole world full of nothing but liars and treacherous brutal vecks that call themselves droogs? Bog blast you, I'll have the lot of you. Where's that bleeding chasso as a like witness?

*The scene explodes into noise – sirens and mouth-whistles. The* **Warder** *comes running in, dousing his fag-end. He does not at first see the body on the floor. He is agitated.*

**Warder**   Get lined up with them brooms. It's the governor and some big bugger coming. Special inspection and not one word of bleeding warning. Jesus. Hey, you, get up.

**Alex**   He can't. He's like snuffed it. These bratchnies here tolchocked him real brutal and nasty.

**The Doctor**   Dear dear dear, Alex. The truth and youth do not go well together, do they?

*There is a fanfare, off but near. The* **Warder** *comes to attention and bawls 'Shun!' The order is obeyed, with* **Jojohn** *and* **Big Jew** *thoughtfully lifting the corpse and holding him upright. Enter the* **Governor** *and the* **Minister of the Interior** *with his aides.*

**Governor**    What's the matter with that man?

**The Doctor** (*suavely*)    Asleep on his feet, sir. He has no bunk. A common complaint in this prison, if I may say so. Overcrowding is an endemic problem.

**Warder** (*loudly*)    You shut your hole when the governor speaks to you.

**Minister**    Well, that's the horse's mouth. The situation is appalling. As he says, an endemic problem. Overcrowding. Common criminals are pre-empting the space we may soon require for political offenders. Well, Gibson, you know the solution.

**Governor**    I have my doubts, Minister. The technique is hardly sufficiently advanced to justify the use of this prison as a –

**Minister**    As a trail-blazer. But there are certain urgencies. Political urgencies, to be candid. And I have every confidence in Brodsky. Common criminals like this unsavoury crowd can best be dealt with on a purely curative basis. Kill the criminal reflex, no more than that. Full implementation in a year's time – that's the government's policy. Punishment means nothing to them, you can see that. They enjoy their so-called punishment. They start murdering each other.

**Jojohn** *and* **Big Jew** *exchange a look, shrug, and then let the body fall.*

**Minister**    Exactly.

**Alex** (*boldly*)    With respect, sir, I object very strongly to what you govoreeted just then. I am not a common criminal, sir, and I am not unsavoury. The others may be unsavoury, but I am not.

**Warder**    You shut your bleeding hole, you. This is the Minister of the Inferior.

**Minister**    Interior. All right, you can start with him. He's young, bold, vicious. Brodsky will deal with him. You can sit in and watch Brodsky. It works all right, don't worry about that. This vicious young hoodlum will be transformed out of all recognition. Tell him about it, will you? Procure the requisite documentation. He might as well start now. All right, I think these creatures may go back to their cells. And this one, of course, may be delivered to the morgue. If there's room. Come, Geoffrey, Cyril.

*He goes off with his aides. The* **Warder** *marches off the prisoners.*

**Governor** (*to* **Warder**)    Knock at the chaplain's door on the way and tell him to come here.

**Warder**    Sir.

*He is off. The* **Governor** *is left alone with* **Alex**, *who stands to attention.*

**Governor**    You, boy, are to be reformed. What's your name?

**Alex**    6655321, sir.

**Governor**    Well, 6655321, you are to go to the famous Dr Brodsky. It is believed that you will be able to leave state custody in a little over two weeks. You will be free again, no longer a number. Does that prospect please you?

**Alex**    Oh, yes, sir. Thank you very much, sir. I've done my best here, really I have. I'm very grateful to all concerned.

**Governor**    Don't be. This is not a reward. This is far from being a reward.

*The* **Chaplain** *enters, with the deliberate step of the drunk. The* **Governor** *nods at him.*

**Governor**    He's to be given the Lodovico Technique. Orders of the Minister of the Interior.

**Chaplain**    God help us.

*The* **Governor** *leaves. The* **Chaplain** *addresses* **Alex** *seriously.*

**Chaplain**    So. You are to be made into a good boy, little 6655321. Never again will you have the desire to commit acts of violence or offend in any way whatsoever against the State's Peace. I hope you take all that in. I hope you are absolutely clear in your own mind about that.

**Alex**    Oh, it will be so nice to be good, sir.

**Chaplain**    It may not be nice to be good, 6655321. It may be horrible to be good. I know I shall have many sleepless nights about this. What does God want? Does God want goodness or the choice of goodness? Is a man who chooses the bad perhaps in some way better than a man who has the good imposed upon him? You are passing now to a region where you will be beyond the power of prayer. A terrible, terrible thing to consider. And yet, in a sense, in choosing to be deprived of the ability to make an ethical choice, you have in a sense really chosen the good. So I shall like to think. So, God help us all, 6655321, I shall like to think.

*He takes out a flat bottle of Scotch and swigs. Then he sobs and sings:*

'God works in a mysterious way
His wonders to perform . . .'

*While he drones on the* **Governor's Secretary** *comes in with forms for* **Alex** *to sign.* **Alex** *signs, grinning with great satisfaction and total misunderstanding of the* **Chaplain**'s *words. The lights dim out. We hear a choral song while the scene changes. The music is that of the first theme of the first movement of Beethoven's Pastoral Symphony:*

In just a fortnight or so
He knows he's going to be free.
(Free as a bee –)
Or a fly or flea.
(Free as the sea)
Or a chestnut tree.

Free free free –
He'll soon be free
(Free as you and me,
If we're truly free –
It's the thing that we
Always want to be –)
In just a fortnight or so
He knows he's going to be free . . .

*The inanity of the words is deliberate. Who the hell knows what freedom is? I don't for one.*

*The lights go up to show a chair and a complex apparatus attached to it.* **Dr Brodsky** *is there with his assistant* **Dr Branom** *(a woman).* **Alex** *is brought on by a white-coated assistant. He is cheerful and polite.*

**Alex**   Morning, all. What was that stuff they shoved into me after breakfast?

**Brodsky**   You enjoyed your breakfast, Alex?

**Alex**   Oh yes, sir. Eggiwegs and lomticks of spik and the old moloko. It was real horrorshow. But what was that –?

**Brodsky**   Vitamins, my boy. You're a little undernourished. Prison diet never did anyone any good. now sit here.

**Alex**   What are you going to do to me, sir?

**Brodsky** *talks as he and* **Branom** *attach wires to his limbs and his carotid artery. They then fix lidlocks to his eyes to keep them open.*

**Brodsky**   You're going to watch some films. And we have dials which will record your reactions to them.

**Alex**   Films? You mean like the sinny? What's these things on my glazzies for, then?

**Brodsky**   To make sure you look. Once close your eyes and the machine fails to register.

**Alex**   But I love the movies, sir. Films are real horrorshow. I *want* to viddy.

**Brodsky**   There's just the possibility that you may – well, we'll see – see being the operative word. His slang – where does he get it from?

**Branom**   Russian and English getting together to make an international teenage patois. Nadsat is the Russian suffix for teen. It's called Nadsat. The two major political languages of the world reduced to an unpolitical jargon –

**Brodsky** (*uninterested*)   Yes yes yes. I think we're ready. Lights. Start.

*The lights go out and a projector flashes from the back of the stage.* **Alex** *sits facing us, weirdly illuminated. We hear atmospheric music, also the noises of beatings, groans, screams, gunshots –*

**Brodsky**   A typical street scene of our time. Vicious teenage hoodlums beating up an old woman. See the blood – it splashes the camera lens. Hear the crack of bones breaking. Now the scene changes. The girl on the pavement is only ten. Her assailants are four in number. The rape is brutal. At the end of it she becomes a thing disposable. Torn to pieces. A gunshot up her –

**Alex** (*in pain*)   No no no.

**Brodsky**   No? But this is the sort of thing you like – you and your generation. (*To* **Branom**.) Reaction eight point seven. Not bad. Now the scene changes once more. A Japanese prison of war camp in World War Two. Torture. A sharp knife disembowels a prisoner live. Now see – a decapitation. Head off as clean as a whistle – see. Headless though he is, the dead man runs around for a short while in total nervous automatism.

**Alex**   No no no. I want to be sick.

**Brodsky**   Ten point four five. A remarkably rapid reaction. All right, lights. Bring him a kidney bowl. Ice-cold water.

*The lights go up.* **Alex** *vomits copiously into a bowl. Exhausted, he drinks water.* **Brodsky** *and* **Branom** *stand near him kindly.*

**Brodsky**    Now then, you're reacting as a normal human being should. Violence is nauseating, and you're – well, nauseated. Flowing in your veins is a chemical substance – patented by the late Dr Lodovico. Dr Lodovico ended his days, alas, as a terminal victim of adolescent mayhem. But his invention marches on.

**Alex**    So it wasn't like – vitamins.

**Brodsky** (*kindly*)    No. It wasn't – like vitamins.

**Alex**    I'm cured. let me out of here. I viddy it all clear as the morning daylight now. It's wrong, wrong and very wrong. Fillying and crasting and tolchocking and the old in-out. I've learned my lesson. I don't need any more.

**Brodsky** (*shocked*)    But the lesson's only just begun.

*The lights dim and, with* **Alex** *groaning, the films are renewed.*

**Brodsky**    Now we see a Nazi concentration camp in which selected Jewish subjects are castrated – without anaesthetic, of course . . .

*His voice is drowned by the entire company, which has assembled on the stage behind* **Alex** *in the near-darkness. They sing the song that opened the act.*

# *Act Two*

*Before the scene is disclosed, we hear the Scherzo of Beethoven's Ninth thumping away, punctuated by the cries of* **Alex** *to stop the music. As the lights come up, we see him as he was at the end of Act One, with the projector flickering and* **Brodsky** *giving a commentary.*

**Brodsky**   Here we see some very recent film – a riot in London's East End, with the police as much responsible for the enormities enacted as the black, brown and white disaffected. Corpses in the gutter, corpses hanging from lampposts, the torn and eviscerated dying. This is the modern world. Sick, sick, mortally sick. 'How like a god,' said Hamlet of humankind. Better to say 'How like a dog'. A dog, as Pavlov showed, can at least be conditioned by the control of its reflexes into behaving like a harmless machine. If mankind is to be saved, science must take over. Science must dig its way into the human brain, crushing the instinct of aggression . . .

**Alex**   All right, all right, but leave him alone. He did no harm. He only did good. It's a sin, it's a sin, I tell you . . .

*And then, his eyes clamped open still, he faints.* **Brodsky** *gets no response from his monitors. He calls.*

**Brodsky**   Lights! Lights! Switch off.

*Lights come up. The projector ceases to project.* **Brodsky**, **Branom** *and the white-coated assistants crowd about* **Alex**. *He is released from the apparatus and brought round with face slapping and a glass of water. He comes to and vomits agonizedly into a bowl. Then, exhausted, he speaks again.*

**Alex**   He did no harm. Why do you punish him?

**Brodsky**   Who?

**Alex**   Beethoven. He gave heaven and you turn it into hell

**Brodsky**   I don't think I quite understand.

**Branom**    That was Beethoven on the sound track. The Scherzo of the Ninth Symphony.

**Brodsky**    Was it? I know nothing about music. I just find it a convenient heightener of emotion, no more.

**Branom**    But surely you see what we've done. Pavlov's dogs salivated when they saw food and heard a bell. Then they salivated when they merely heard the bell. Withdraw the images of violence while keeping the musical accompaniment – he'll respond in the same way. Not salivating, of course – vomiting. From now on music will make him vomit. Did you foresee this?

**Brodsky**    No, but does it matter? Music's a discardable luxury – like marijuana or cheap sweets. It's the quelling of the violent impulse that matters. I think he's cured.

**Branom**    No. We've given him a new disease. Music was once the way into heaven. He used the right words. Now it's going to be hell. I think, Dr Brodsky, I want to withdraw from the experiment. I'd be happy if you'd omit my name from the reports. You've bitten off far far more than you can chew.

*Saying which, she tears off her white coat and leaves.* **Brodsky** *looks at her leaving, doubtful, but then he smiles manically at* **Alex**.

**Brodsky**    You feel all right now? (**Alex** *nods warily.*) Have you noticed a small but vital change in procedure these last few days?

**Alex** *thinks, then speaks.*

**Alex**    You've not been giving me those injections.

**Brodsky**    No. There's no need for them any more. You've been permanently inoculated. The distaste for violence has been programmed into your biochemistry. My forecast has proved correct. To the day, to the minute. Take him away. Inform the distinguished gentlemen – and, of course, the ah professional participants – that all is ready.

*To music there is an arranging of chairs by the white-coated assistants.*
*A dais is wheeled on. The* **Governor**, *the* **Minister of the**
**Interior**, *the* **Prison Chaplain** *come in, as also warders and*
*other interested officials. The audience becomes a specially convened*
*body.*

**Minister**    Take your seats, please. No noise. Try not to
cough.

*He sings the following, to the music of the slow movement of*
*Beethoven's Fifth Symphony.*

> With some pride Government presents
> The end-result of Government's experiments.
> They said that I'm
> To concentrate
> On the crime
> Rate.

**Chorus**
> On the crime rate.

**Minister**
> I'm only here to serve.
> I steeled my nerve
> With what results you'll observe.

**Chorus**
> Let us observe.

**Minister**
> Give us the votes we deserve.

**Chorus**
> We will vote you back in like responsive adults
> When we see –

**Minister**
> Yes?

**Chorus**
> When we see –

**Minister**

Yes?

**Chorus**

Positive results.

*The theme blazes on the orchestra as* **Alex** *walks in uncertainly. He wears his old platties of the nochy – the only clothes he brought in with him. They provoke titters.*

**Minister**    Aha. Now, ladies and gentlemen, we introduce the subject himself. Today we send him with confidence out into the world again, as decent a lad as you would meet on a May morning, inclined to the kindly word and the helpful act. What a change is here from the wretched hoodlum the State committed to unprofitable punishment some two years ago, unchanged after two years. Unchanged, do I say? Not quite. Prison taught him the false smile, the rubbed hands of hypocrisy, the fawning greased obsequious leer. Other vices it taught him too, as well as confirming him in those he had long practised before. But, ladies and gentlemen, enough of words. Actions speak louder than. Action now. Observe, all.

**Alex** *has been led to the dais, on which a spotlight is trained. There is music appropriate to a comic stage act. A* **Comedian** *walks in to work on* **Alex**.

**Comedian**    Hello, heap of dirt. Pooh, you don't wash much, do you, judging from the horrible pong.

*He stamps on* **Alex**'s *feet, flicks his nose painfully, twists his ear.* **Alex** *is surprised.*

**Alex**    What do you do that to me for, bratty? I've never done like wrong to you, brother.

**Comedian**    Oh, I do this and that and those (*He repeats his aggressive gestures.*) because I don't care for your horrible type, and if you want to do something about it, please do.

**Alex** *makes as to attack back, but he feels like vomiting. He takes out his razor and feels even more like it as he sees it shining in the light.*

**Alex**   I'd like to give you a cancer, brother, but I don't seem to have any. Take this instead. A real horrorshow britva.

**Comedian**   Keep your stinking bribes to yourself. You can't get round me that way.

*He bangs on* **Alex***'s hand and the razor clatters to the boards. He continues to dance around* **Alex** *like a boxer, hitting, kicking.* **Alex** *is desperate.*

**Alex**   Please, brother, I must do something. Shall I clean your boots? Look, I'll get down and do it with my yahzick –

*And he crouches and starts to lick the* **Comedian***'s boots with his tongue. The* **Comedian** *kicks out.* **Alex** *instinctively grasps his legs and brings him hurtling down. The audience laughs but* **Alex** *feels sick and tries to vomit. But nothing comes up. The* **Comedian** *prepares to give* **Alex** *a really earnest punch, but the* **Minister** *intervenes.*

**Minster**   Thank you, that will do very well.

*The* **Comedian** *bows to applause professionally, implicating* **Alex** *in the act with a generous gesture. Then he dances off.* **Brodsky***, at a nod from the* **Minister***, addresses the audience.*

**Brodsky**   Our subject is, you see, impelled towards the good by, paradoxically, being impelled towards evil. The intention to act violently is accompanied by strong feelings of physical distress. To counter these the subject has to switch to a diametrically opposed attitude. Any questions?

**Chaplain**   Choice. He has no real choice, has he? Self-interest, fear of physical pain, drove him to that grotesque act of self-abasement. Its insincerity was clearly to be seen. He ceases to be a wrongdoer. He ceases also to be a creature capable of moral choice.

**Brodsky** (*smiling*)   These are subtleties. We are not concerned with the higher ethics. We are concerned only with cutting down crime.

**Minister**    And with relieving the ghastly congestion in our prisons.

**Governor** (*with a sour look at his chaplain*)    Hear hear.

**Chorus** (*chattersinging to the second variation of the main theme of the Beethoven slow movement already heard*)

It's an experiment that really seems to work
It's quite amazing all the elements that lurk
Below the surface dedicated to destroy
Can be subdued it's quite essential to employ
This new device to keep the social structure pure
Of criminality and so help to secure
A glowing future in which villainy will seem
A tale for kids or else the memory of a dream . . .

**Alex** (*cutting in loudly*)    Me, me, me. How about me? Where do I come in into all this? Am I just like some animal or dog? Am I to be just like a clockwork orange?

*The term is new to the auditors and it shuts them up. But a* **Voice** *from the auditorium speaks.*

**Voice**    You have no cause to grumble, boy. Whatever now ensues is what you yourself have chosen.

**Chaplain**    Oh, if only I could believe that. He's been transformed into a mere engine, fuelled by fear, incapable of hate, choice, worship or even human love.

**Chorus**    Love? *Love?* LOVE? *LOVE?*

**Minister** (*smiling*)    I am glad this question of Love has been raised. Now we shall see in action a manner of Love that was thought to be dead with the middle ages.

*To music (preferably this same slow movement) a most beautiful* **Girl**, *near nude, makes her sidling entrance. A sharp intake of breath from all the men present.* **Alex**'s *response is complex. He makes towards her with his arms out, fired by sheer lust. But he starts to vomit and has to screech out as follows.*

**Alex**   O most beautiful and beauteous of devotchkas. I throw like my ticker at your feet for you to like trample over. If I had a red red rose I would give it to you. If it was all rainy and cally you could have my platties to walk on so as not to cover your dainty nogas with filth and cal. Let me worship you and be like your helper and protector from the wicked like world. Let me be like your true knight.

*And he grovels. The* **Girl** *bows and dances off to applause.*

**Brodsky**   He will be your true Christian. Ready to turn the other cheek. Ready to be crucified rather than crucify. Sick to the very heart at the thought even of killing a fly.

*He looks carefully at* **Alex** *to see his response to the notion of fly-killing.* **Alex** *dutifully starts to vomit.*

**Chorus**
   Let the heavens rejoice
   At this comforting voice.
   We've destroyed
   (Overjoyed)
   Liberty of choice.

**Minister**   The point is that it works.

**Chaplain**   Oh, it works all right, God help the lot of us.

*The scene ends.*

*The scene is now the vestibule of a flatblock – garnished with graffiti and rubbish.* **Alex**, *self-conscious in his bizarre get-up, waits, moving up and down, trying to keep warm. It is a chilly winter evening. A* **Woman** *comes out to throw rubbish in a dustbin. She looks at* **Alex** *suspiciously.*

**Woman**   What you want here then?

**Alex**   I live here. Got no key, though. Waiting, you know. For my dad. Or mum. Or both. Coming home from work. You know.

**Woman**   Yeah. (*She takes a closer look at* **Alex**.) Seen you before somewhere. Wait. (*She rummages among the rubbish she*

writer, you know. F. Alexander is the name. Perhaps you have heard it.

*While talking, he brings on a card table and a chair and sets them up.* **Alex** *takes off his torn clothes, wincing, and dons the dressing gown.*

**Alex**    The name Alexander I know, sir. It is like my own eemya, sir.

**Alexander** *(alert)*    What? What's that?

*He takes from the pocket of the raincoat he is too absentminded to have taken off a newspaper. He looks at it. He looks at* **Alex.**

**Alexander**    It is you. 'Alex number one guinea pig of government criminal reform scheme. Badness burnt out by Brodsky. Minister of Interior looks with confidence towards new crime-free era . . .' It is you, poor victim. Providence bade me pick you up in your blood. The victim, but also a weapon.

**Alex**    Weapon? I don't quite pony that, sir.

**Alexander**    Deprived of choice. A man who cannot choose ceases to be a man. This overbearing evil government. To turn a decent young boy into a piece of clockwork. They will do it to us all. Censorship is on its way. My writings are already suspect. Since the death of my poor wife I have given my life to fighting the evil that is abroad. And this government tries to stamp out evil with a worse evil. The book I wrote – itself a double victim. The manuscript torn up by the wretched villains who then tore up my wife. The published book banned.

**Alex** *(to whom it all comes back)*    Oh God. What was the book called, sir?

**Alexander**    It is still called *A Clockwork Orange.* Man is a fruit, a creature of juice and colour and perfume. They would tear out his pith and turn him into a robot. They will try to do it to us all. But you, poor victim, shall be a witness against them.

**Alex** (*somewhat shaken*)    You said. Something. About. A wife. Sir.

**Alexander**    She died. She was brutally ravished and beaten. The shock was very great. She always had a weak heart. She did not survive a month.

*Suddenly broken, sobbing, he sits on the chair he placed at the card table. He delivers the following speechsong, based on the Adagio of Beethoven's Ninth.* **Alex** *fights with the desire to vomit, trying to force certain events out of his memory.*

She was all things to me,
She was my body and brain –
Her hair was sheaves of autumn,
Her smile was midsummer rain.
She was all springs to me,
The earth renewed every day.
The leaves come green in April.
Though they
Fall in the fall and burn.
She will not return.

Often in dreams I hear her
(I'm standing near her)
– She shakes her head.
'The futility of anger,
The sin of vengeance –
How can these profit the dead?'
But if they were here –
I'm living still –
My living will
Would seek to break, to rend, to kill –
Useless, useless, as she said.

She was all springs to me,
The earth renewed every day.
The leaves come green in April.
Though they
Fall in the fall and burn.
She will not return.

*There is a knock at the door.* **Alexander** *is bewildered, but then his face clears.*

**Alexander**    Of course. Today is Wednesday. I'd forgotten. I forget everything. My wife was my – memory.

*So saying, he opens up and lets in two men – Messrs* **Dolin** *and* **Rubinstein**. *They too are shabby, but they are clothed in the flame of political idealism.*

**Alexander**    This is – I've forgotten your name.

**Alex**    Alex.

**Dolin**    Good God – how did you get him?

**Alexander** (*bewildered*)    You know him? Oh – you mean you read. Yes yes. Opportune. I see that. Heavens, yes. I never thought.

**Rubinstein**    So for once our meeting has teeth. God – his presence sets my brain whirring like clockwork. What a superb device he could be. He could for preference look even iller and more zombyish than he does. No doubt we can think of something.

**Alex**    What goes on, bratties? What dost thou in thy razodock for thy little droog have?

**Alexander**    Eh? Eh? That manner of voice pricks me. I heard it before. Once before.

**Dolin**    Public meetings. A ruined life is the approach. We must inflame all hearts.

**Alex**    And what is in this veshch for me, brothers? Tortured in jail, thrown out by my own pee and em and a bolshy brutal like lodger, near-killed by the millicents – And even if I slooshy lovely music –

**Dolin**    Yes?

**Alex**    I want to sick up.

**Rubinstein**    Interesting interesting. I read that interview with the defecting Dr Branom. Not conditioning, she said – overconditioning.

**Alex**    There's only one veshch I require, and that's to be normal and healthy as I was in the starry days, having my malenky bit of twenty to one with real droogs and not those grahzny bratchnies who are like traitors. Can you do that? Can you restore me to what I was is what I want to like know.

**Dolin**    The Party will not be ungrateful, boy. A martyr to the cause of liberty. You have your part to play in the overthrow of this damnable repressive government.

*He strokes* **Alex** *as if he were a toy.* **Alex** *cries out.*

**Alex**    I'm not a thing, brother. I'm not one of your ordinary prestoopniks and like criminals. I'm not ordinary and I'm not dim. Do you slooshy?

**Alexander**    Dim. Dim. That was a name somewhere. Dim.

**Alex**    Eh? What's Dim to do with it? What do you know about Dim? Oh, Bog help us.

**Alexander**    I could almost believe – But such things are impossible. For, by Christ, if he were I'd tear him, I'd split him, by God, yes, so I would –

**Dolin**    There there. It's all in the past. It was other people altogether. We must help this poor victim. He must help us. Look to the future. Look to the cause. Let him sleep here. Tomorrow we start work. In earnest. Come. We've things to discuss.

**Alexander** *looks doubtfully at* **Alex**, *who looks fearfully back, but suffers himself to be led out.* **Alex**, *alone, starts to retch. His mouth bulging, he rushes to a receptacle.*

*The lights go down. The first movement of Beethoven's Ninth begins and continues through the scene that follows. The lights come up gradually – as in a speeded up dawn – to show* **Alex** *in his underclothes or even naked lying on the floor mattress. He wakes to hear the music. Strong feelings of distress begin. He gets up, looks for the source of the music. He thinks it is coming from the floor above. He screams 'Stop it, stop it' to no avail. He tried to get out, but the door is locked. There is a curtain upstage. He draws this back to disclose a window. He holds his head in desperation, moans, screams, finally tries to knock himself senseless by banging his skull on the floor. The music continues. He picks up a newspaper. Its headline states: 'DEATH TO TYRANNY'. He is confirmed in his bid for suicide. He goes to the window.*

**Alex** (*to the audience*)    Goodbye. May Bog forgive you for a ruined jeezny.

*He leaps out of the window. We hear his screams as he falls. The music, indifferent as heaven, continues. The lights fade. No music introduces the next scene.*

*The next scene is in a hospital. It is an empty ward, no beds, merely two doctors examining files. One of the two is* **Branom**.

**Branom**    No physiological problems. Orthopedically a success. What concerns us, of course, is the possibility that the physical trauma may have undone Brodsky's conditioning.

**Other Doctor**    You want that to happen? After all your own work in the Pavlovian Institute?

**Branom**    The cause of this boy's near death has been well and accurately publicized. He tried to kill himself to escape from the music of Beethoven.

**Other Doctor**    I don't care much for Beethoven myself. Still, that was going too far. Sorry, Dr Branom. How soon can you tell?

**Branom**    I think he's already capable of submitting to a few tests. Perhaps later today.

*She presses a wall-switch.*

**Other Doctor**    And the political angle?

**Branom**    What do you mean?

**Other Doctor**    Whatever you do you're caught up in the political angle. The government wanted one thing. Now it wants another. But it's still the same government. And the same Minister of the Interior of Inferior.

**Branom**    There are some issues which are bigger than politics. Ah, here he is.

**Alex** *is wheeled in on his bed. He is bandaged totally, except for a portion of his face, and one leg is suspended. A* **Nurse** *is with him.*

**Branom**    Let him sleep. Tell me when he wakes up, nurse.

*The lights dim and soft music sounds.* **Alex** *dreams. He sees the figure of the* **Prison Chaplain**, *drunk but dressed in angelic white. He carries newspapers.*

**Chaplain**    You see the headlines, little 6655321 as used to be? BOY VICTIM OF CRIMINAL REFORM SCHEME. GOVERNMENT AS MURDERER. OUT OUT OUT. That means the government. Religion is above politics, so I believed. But now I see how the two conjoin. It is all a matter of freedom of choice. We have the right to choose evil. Have we? Have we? Can I preach that from any pulpit? Better if I go into retirement. I have received a very tempting offer from a distillery.

*So saying, he tears off his white robe and reveals a natty suit. His image fades.* **Alex** *comes to. He addresses the* **Nurse** *who sits by his bed.*

**Alex**    What gives, O my little sister? Come thou and have a nice lay down with your malenky droog on this bed.

*The* **Nurse** *starts up and rings the bell. She runs out.*

**Nurse**    Doctor! Doctor! He's awake.

**Branom** *and her assistant come in.* **Branom** *carries a picture book. She comes over to* **Alex** *and speaks gently.*

**Branom**    This won't take long. I'm going to show you some pictures. While you're looking at one, say exactly what comes into your mind. All right?

**Alex**    Rightirightiright.

**Branom**    This first one. It's a bird's nest. Full of eggs.

**Alex**    Very very nice. Real horrorshow.

**Branom**    And what would you like to do about it?

**Alex**    Smash them. Pick up the lot and like smash them against a wall or a cliff and then viddy them all smash up real horrorshow.

*Both doctors show approval. The* **Other Doctor** *makes a tick on a list.*

**Branom**    This picture is of a peacock. You've seen them, haven't you? Look at its lovely tail spread out in a beautiful fan.

**Alex**    I would like to pull out like all those feathers in its tail and slooshy it creech blue murder. For being so like boastful.

**Branom**    And this lovely young girl?

**Alex**    Give her the old in-out in-out real savage with lots of ultra-violence.

**Branom**    And this scene of looting and killing in east London?

**Alex**    I'd like to put the boot straight in everybody's litso and viddy the old red red krovvy spurting out.

**Branom**    Good. And this rather holy picture?

**Alex**    The old nagoy droog of the prison charlie carrying his cross up a hill. I'd like to hammer in the old nails bang

bang. Bang. Two for his rookers, one for his nogas. And one for luck in the gulliver.

**Branom**    I think that's enough. You seem to be cured.

**Alex**    Cured? Me tied down to this bed and you say cured? Kiss my sharries is what I govoreet like in reply.

*Not only the* **Nurse** *but the* **Matron** *come in in great urgency. The* **Matron** *whispers something to* **Branom**, *and the* **Nurse** *tidies up* **Alex**'s *bed.*

**Branom**    Already?

*Photographers come in, cameras and flashes ready. Then there is a fanfare, and the* **Minister of the Interior** *appears, with his aides.*

**Alex**    The Minister of the Inferior in poison. Well well well well well. What giveth then, old droogie?

**Aide**    Speak more respectfully, boy, when addressing a minister of the Crown.

**Alex**    Yarbles. Bolshy great yarblockos to thee and thine.

**Minister**    All right all right. He speaks to me as a friend, don't you, son?

**Alex**    I am everybody's friend. Except to my enemies.

**Minister**    And who are your enemies? Tell us that, my boy.

**Alex**    All who do me wrong are my enemies.

**Minister**    Well, I and the government of which I am a member want you to regard us as friends. Yes, friends. We have put you right, yes? You are getting the best of treatment. We never wished you harm, but there are some who did and do. And I think you know who those are. They wished to use you for base political ends. They would have been glad to see you dead for those ends and then blame it on the government. I think you know who those men are. There is a man named F. Alexander, a writer of subversive literature, who has been howling for your blood. He has been mad with desire to stick a knife in you. But you're safe from him now. We had him put away.

**Alex**   He was supposed to be like a droog. Like a droog he was supposed to be.

**Minister**   He believed you had done most bitter wrong to someone near his heart.

**Alex**   You mean that he was like told.

**Minister**   He had this idea. He was a menace. So we put him away.

**Alex**   Kind. Most kind of thou.

**Minister**   When you leave here you will have no worries. We shall see to everything. Because you are helping us.

**Alex**   Am I?

**Minister**   We always help our friends, don't we?

*He sits on the bed and puts his arm about* **Alex**. *Photographers shout 'Smile!' and click and flash away.*

**Minister**   Good boy. Good good boy. And now, see, a present.

*A* **Man** *in a white coat supervises the bringing in of an expensive stereo set. He carries an armful of cassettes.*

**Man**   What shall it be? Mozart? Benjy Britt? Schoenberg? Carl Orff?

**Alex**   The Ninth. The glorious Ninth.

**Man**   Thought so. All ready in.

*The last movement sounds. The* **Man** *exchanges a conspiratorial glance with the* **Minister**. **Alex** *is offered a document to sign. He signs without looking. He is absorbed in the music. His eyes close.* **Branom** *addresses him.*

**Branom**   What do you see?

**Alex**    I can viddy myself very clear running and running on like very light and mysterious nogas, carving the whole litso of the creeching world with my cut-throat britva.

**Branom**    You're cured all right.

**Alex**    Yeah. Cured all right.

*The scene ends, but not the play.*

*The scene is the Korova (Russian for cow by the way, if anyone's interested) Milk Bar as in the opening scene.* **Alex**, *visibly older, even with an incipient moustache, is with three new droogs. They are named* **Rick**, **Len** *and* **Bully**. *These three sing the song that opened Act One, but* **Alex** *sits apart, a little bored.*

**Bully**    Well, then, droogie, thou being the oldest and like the leader, what dost thou in mind for this kolodnyiy winter nochy like have?

**Alex**    Look, droogies. Tonight I am somehow just not in like the mood. I know not why or how it is, but there it is. You three go your own ways this nightwise, leaving me out out and out. On my oddy knocky. Tomorrow we shall meet same place same time, me hoping to be like a lot better. Right? Rightiright?

**Bully**    Too tough a day like, is that it? In the old Music Archives, gloopy sort of a naz.

**Alex**    The polly's horrorshow.

**Bully**    Yeah? Pretty polly grows on trees, old droogie. Only a bezoomny shoot does rabbiting for it. Horrorshow, right. If you won't itty with us, right sorry I am.

**Alex**    You're not sorry, Bully boy. I viddy the old look in your glazzy – power, power and power. Well, take it. Heil, tovarish. Itty off and about. And the very best of.

*All three make lip shooms at* **Alex**, *give him the finger, and dance off. As soon as they have gone,* **Alex** *adjusts his gear. He takes off his yellow wig, disclosing decently barbed hair. He puts on a stylish cravat.*

*He is ready for the pretty young girl who now hurries in to meet him. Her name is* **Marty**.

**Marty**    Sorry I'm late. We were a bit rushed in the shop.

**Alex**    No need for sorrow. Glad to see you, Marty, and very glad. Sit. What will it be? The old moloko?

**Marty**    You do talk funny sometimes. You mean milk?

**Alex**    Vaccine secretion. Cow juice. (*He clicks his fingers. Two glasses of milk are eventually brought. No hurry.*) Did you think on what I said?

**Marty**    We're both too young. Me seventeen. You eighteen.

**Alex**    Not too molodoy. Sorry. At least think. I mean, it's you and me together, right?

**Marty**    Right if you like.

**Alex**    Not so young, though. Me. Not so young as I was. Old Wolfgang Amadeus had done a lot at my age. Felix M. too. And Benjy Britt. Not so young. Old enough to know that being young is like being an animal. No, it's more like being one of those malenky toys you viddy being sold in the street, made out of tin with a spring inside and a handle, and you wind it up grrr grrr grrr and off it itties in a straight line and bangs straight into things bang bang and doesn't pony what it's doing. That's being young. And the ultra-violence and the fillying and the crasting – that's being young too. I'm growing up. I look to the future and a son of my own who'll make the same mistakes as I did just because he'll be young.

**Marty**    You still talk funny. And you're jumping ahead a bit, aren't you?

**Alex**    Life's not very long. Think about it.

**Marty**    I'll think.

**Alex**   I was doing this job in the State Music Archives today, and I was cataloguing the ten new recordings of the Ninth. And words kept on ittying through my gulliver.

**Marty**   There you go again.

**Alex**   You want to slooshy? Hear, that is.

*She nods. He sings.*

> Being young's a sort of sickness,
> Measles, mumps or chicken pox.
> Gather all your toys together
> Lock them in an iron box.
> That means tolchocks, crasting and dratsing,
> All of the things that suit a boy.
> When you build instead of busting,
> You can start your Ode to Joy.

*The other characters of the play come on at the back, friendly as at a party, while* **Alex** *comes downstage and speaks to the audience.*

**Alex**   That's how it going to be, brothers, as we come to the end of this like tale. You have been everywhere with your little droog Alex, suffering with him, and you have viddied some of the most grahzny bratchnies old Bog ever made, all on to your old droog Alex. And all it was was that I was young. I am not young, not no longer, ah no. Alex like groweth up, ah yes. Tomorrow is all like sweet flowers and the turning vonny earth, like a juicy orange in the gigantic rookers of Bog. And there's the stars and the old Luna up there and your old droog Alex growing up. A terrible grahzny vonny world really, brothers and sisters. And so farewell from your little droog. And to all others in this story – except one, and you've just met her – profound shooms of lip music brrrrrrrr. And they can kiss my sharries. But you – remember sometimes thy little Alex that was. Amen. And all that cal.

*He joins with the entire company in singing the following. A man bearded like Stanley Kubrick comes on playing, in exquisite counterpoint, 'Singin' in the Rain' on a trumpet. He is kicked off the stage.*

Do not be a clockwork orange,
Freedom has a lovely voice.
Here is good, and there is evil –
Look on both, then take your choice.
Sweet in juice and hue and aroma,
Let's not be changed to fruit machines.
Choice is free but seldom easy –
That's what human freedom means!

*End.*

# A CLOCKWORK ORANGE

## 1. PRELUDE

Come prima

ACT ONE

## 2. Alex and Droogs

Molto Moderato

What's it going to be then, eh? . . . . . .

What's it going to be then, eh? . . . .

# Allegro

as in text P. 2.

Moderato

what's it going to be then, eh? ....

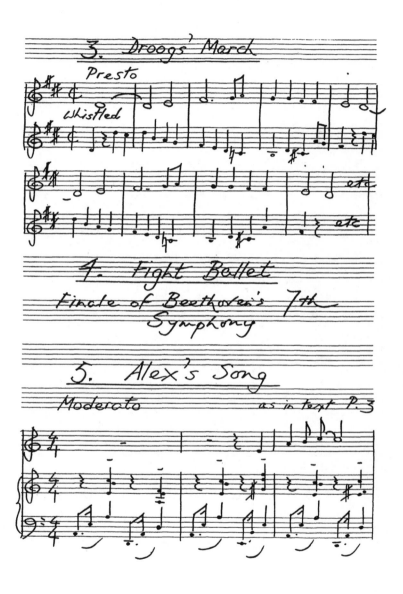

(bleat)

# 7. Droogs' Chorus

### p. 5

8. Jukebox Song

p. 6

Slow & Dreamy

repeat ad lib.

## 9. What Gets Into You?

(Mr Deltoid)

Slow     P. 7

Alex:

ALEX: (P. 8)

teaching us

# 10.  Prisoners' Hymn

## 11. Discipline

P. 16

Easy

13. Reprise No. 2

END OF ACT ONE

## ACT TWO

### 13 Minister and Chorus

13a
Chatter Chorus
P. 30

It's an ex-    Work

# 13 b.
## Chorus

Maestoso        p. 31

Let the heavens rejoice

14. She Was
All Things to Me   P. 37

_lacrimoso_

All springs to me ....

## 15. FINALE

During Alex's monologue

Kick trumpeter off